LONELY PLANET'S
BEST EVER
TRAVEL
Tips

LONELY PLANET'S
BEST EVER
TRAVEL

Tips

BY TOM HALL

**GET THE BEST TRAVEL
SECRETS & ADVICE FROM
THE EXPERTS**

**FIND THE BEST
VALUE DEALS**

**SCORE THAT
ELUSIVE UPGRADE**

**STAY SAFE
ON THE ROAD**

CONTENTS

TOP 50 TRAVEL TIPS

QUICK-REFERENCE TRAVEL HACKS

INTRODUCTION

For a travel geek, the prospect of putting together a book like this is a dream assignment: attempt to distill all the important travel knowledge in the world into 50 individual, bitesized tips. While making sure they're not too obvious – 'don't sit in the sun until you turn the colour of a lobster' is not much of a tip – there's also a need to avoid topics that are too obscure, so there are no guidelines here on how to pilot a husky or map the backwaters of Pohnpei's lagoon canals.

The aim is to pass on universal advice that you can take with you wherever in the world you go

One way to approach this challenge is to break the world of travel into various subjects, and find an expert who can talk knowledgeably about each one. We've spoken to several dozen seriously clued-up travel experts about everything from technology to adventure, and urban exploration to connecting with local people and other travellers. The aim with *Best Ever Travel Tips* is to pass on universal advice that you can take with you wherever in the world you go, and whatever budget you travel at. And if we pass on a trade secret or two then we, and we're sure you, won't mind at all.

Tom Hall

TOP
50

TRAVEL TIPS

THE BEST TIME TO BOOK FLIGHTS TO GET THE BEST RATES
FAQs for beating the system

When do tickets go on sale for flights?

Usually, 11 months in advance. Reasons for this are arcane and historical – in the days of printed seat plans, airlines wanted to avoid booking people on to the right plane, on the right day, in the wrong year.

So should you charge in and book almost a year ahead?

Not normally. Airlines can (and often do) update fares every hour using complex algorithms. This is the dark art of yield management – trying to get the fullest planes, with passengers paying as much as possible for every seat.

So when is the best time?

There are certain broad trends: on average the best time is five weeks before travel. If you have time it can pay to watch your route carefully and educate yourself about when cheaper seats are generally available – varying day of departure and time of day can make a big difference.

What about if you're flying at a very busy time, like over Christmas?

This may be the time to book very early: all fare classes will be available, and you should score a price that won't be beatable nearer the time. You'll also ensure you get a seat on the plane you want.

Filip Filipov, Head of B2B, Skyscanner

ALWAYS GET THE BEST PRICE ON AN AIRLINE SEAT
How to bag a bargain in an airline sale

- -

When the need to fill seats meets the recent explosion in capacity on key international routes – driven by recent expansion by Middle Eastern and Asian carriers – passengers can, in theory, pick up great deals on seat sales.

1 'As a general rule carriers will have a January sale and a September sale,' says Stuart Lodge from roundtheworldflights. com. 'Airlines are trying to fill seats for the next "shoulder season" – March to May for the first sale, and October and November in the second. Sales aren't unheard of outside this time, but they're certainly less frequent.'

2 If you're travelling during school holidays or other peak periods, there's no point waiting for a sale – you just won't get the deals.

3 By definition, seat sales target routes with sluggish sales. A high-demand, low capacity route is less likely to feature in a sale.

4 Airlines often follow each other's lead in sales, which can cause domino effects in discounting. It's not unusual to have half a dozen airlines on sale at once.

5 Sign up for email alerts and social media accounts from airlines to find out about sales. This is generally how airlines announce sales.

BAG THE ULTIMATE ROUND-THE-WORLD TICKET

Stuart Lodge from roundtheworldflights.com offers tips for getting the most from the biggest ticket you can buy

Decide to go

Travel between mid-April and June to get the best prices, or at least avoid peak travel times – July, August, December and January. By travelling east to west at this time you'll also follow the best weather around the world.

Decide where

Most people structure their trip around two or three of their must-see destinations. Be aware that adding South America generally adds complexity and cost.

Know the rules

Most people make several changes after their initial booking. Flexible tickets cost more at purchase, but will save you money in the long term.

Know when not to use your ticket

Some countries, such as Indonesia and many places in South America, are popular without being well-served by RTW tickets. In these cases it's cheaper and easier to get to a nearby hub and hop on a low-cost flight, then rejoin your RTW later.

Land ho

Open sections of RTW tickets allow for a mammoth train ride to see the world from ground level. If you're finding the trail well-worn, deviate from the norm by drawing a 'v' rather than a straight line between a and b.

FIVE TIPS FOR TRAVELLING LIGHT
Doug Dyment – travel speaker, go-light guru and author of OneBag.com

1 There's only one real 'secret' to travelling light: a proper personal packing list. It's a contract you make with yourself, a personal pledge that you will never pack anything in that isn't on your list. And for most people, such a list, able to accommodate destinations ranging from India to Inuvik, needn't hold more items than will fit in a single, carry-on-sized bag.

2 Learn about luggage. Most bags on the market are designed to sell easily, not facilitate lightweight travel. So learn about design (shapes, configurations) and construction (fabrics, zippers). You may even discover that the primary function of a wheeled bag is to support itself, not efficiently transport anyone's belongings!

3 Avoid liquids; they are the bane of the light traveller. Liquids (and gels) are heavy, bulky, prone to leakage (particularly on planes), and suspicious to security. Did I mention heavy?

4 Do some laundry. This needn't be onerous: done properly, and regularly, it's more like brushing your teeth than a major chore. With the right gear (traveller's clothes line, powder detergent, universal sink stopper), three pairs of underwear will take you anywhere.

5 Coordinate your colours. An excellent way to derive maximum use from a modest amount of clothing is to ensure that every item goes with every other one.

5

GROUND
WORK

PRE-DEPARTURE CHECKLIST
Don't leave home without getting the essentials in check

Your passport
OK, you've probably thought of this one already – but check the expiry date. Some countries require at least six months' validity. And if you have to renew, make sure you leave plenty of time, especially during peak periods. You can check if a visa is required at www.iatatravelcentre.com.

Pre-book and save
Book in advance before getting to the airport for parking and holiday money. Even if you do so on the morning of your trip you'll save. If picking up pre-booked currency, take the card you booked with and take note if you have to go to a particular pickup point to get your cash.

Get insured – and 'fess up
Travel insurance is mostly health insurance, which is why the cost increases hugely when you get to retirement age. For it to be effective every pre-existing condition must be declared – otherwise your policy could be worthless and you could end up with a very large bill.

Missing in action
Lost baggage that never gets reunited with its owners either ends up being auctioned off or, in the USA, at the Unclaimed Luggage Centre in Scottsborough, Alabama (www.unclaimedbaggage.com).

COVERED!
What to look for in a travel insurance policy

Travel insurance will hopefully be something you don't have to worry about at all when travelling – but it is certainly something you need to sort out before you leave.

1 **Be covered for where you're going**
This sounds obvious, but check that your cover will apply where you're going, especially if you're visiting popular destinations just outside what may be considered Europe, like Morocco and Turkey.

2 **...and what you're doing** Attempting to ski? Trying climbing? Make sure your cover extends to that. Read the policy carefully to see if there are restrictions relating to, for example, going off-piste.

3 **How much cover?** It may seem like your medical provision amounts to mind-boggling millions that you will never need, but remember this is worst-case-scenario stuff. The highest levels of cover are worth it if you're going to the USA, where health care is expensive.

4 **Take your documents – and a copy**
Travel with your insurance documents, and also have a copy on email you can access. Make sure you store the contact number of your insurer in your phone.

5 **Drinking and insurance don't mix**
Certain policies will be invalid if you are drunk or under the influence of drugs, so go easy when on the road.

THE ULTIMATE CLOTHES-PACKING TIP
Learn the art of bundle wrapping

GROUND
WORK

Few travel moments are more discouraging than having one's carefully packed clothing emerge at the destination a wrinkled mess. And there's really only one consistently effective solution. Surprisingly, not that many people have learned how to do it.

The twin goals are to eliminate folding (which creates creases), and prevent garments from sliding against one another (the source of wrinkles). All hail a technique called 'bundle wrapping', the careful wrapping of clothes around a central core object (perhaps a flat pouch stuffed with socks and underwear).

Position easily-rumpled clothing (jackets, shirts) further from the core, and more forgiving items (sweaters, slacks) closer to the centre. Secure the resulting bundle against shifting, using the tie-down straps in your suitcase.

You'll need some more detail, and it's a skill much better illustrated than described (search for 'bundle wrapping' on the internet), but one well worth learning. Even that dressy linen outfit can be included in your travel plans.

Doug Dyment – travel speaker, go-light guru and author of OneBag.com

THINGS AN AIRLINE PILOT KNOWS ABOUT TRAVEL

Insider tips on getting from a to b

Pack smart

A large part of my job is about routine, and packing is no different. I have individual positions for each important item in my carry-on bag (passport, wallet, phone, etc) so I know where to find it and, more importantly, whether it's missing.

Pick your timings

If travelling a primarily north or south long-haul route with few or no time zone changes, I highly recommend a daylight flight that departs in the morning. You'll arrive in the evening and have a good night's rest, waking up fresh the next day. Doing the same flight overnight is a different story.

Be prepared

In the very unlikely event of an emergency, you need to be mobile and ready for anything. There's nothing wrong with taking your shoes off and changing mid-flight, but during take-off and landing always wear long pants and a good pair of shoes.

Stay hydrated

For long-haul flights I can't stress enough the importance of hydration, not just during but before and after the flight. So avoid caffeinated drinks, as well as alcohol. I don't leave home without a bit of lip balm: cracked lips and long flights go hand in hand.

Andrew Pascoe, commercial pilot

FREIGHTER TRAVEL 101
Hop aboard a cargo ship for a unique and green alternative to flying

These mighty vessels sail between the world's container ports and several shipping firms are happy to bring a limited amount of SLF (self-loading freight, or passengers to you and I) along for the ride. Forget working your passage: you'll pay your way no matter how handy you are with paintbrush or broom.

Journeys on freighters aren't cruises. Passengers are left to their own devices to while away the days, and mealtimes are simple affairs, taken with the crew. When in port, which is usually a long way from city centres and often not in desperately desirable parts of the world, passengers need to make their own arrangements to have a look around.

Sailings are good value – costing around US$130 per day at sea – and you'll often need to book up to a year or more in advance. Want to know more? In the US, try TravLTips (www.travltips.com); Cruise People (www.cruisepeople.co.uk) are a UK expert; and Freighter Travel NZ (www.freightertravel.co.nz) throughout Australia, NZ and the Pacific.

Where planes can't fly

Does your bucket list include places you can only reach by boat? Their numbers are dwindling but try St Helena and Tristan da Cunha in the southern Atlantic Ocean and Pitcairn Island in the Pacific.

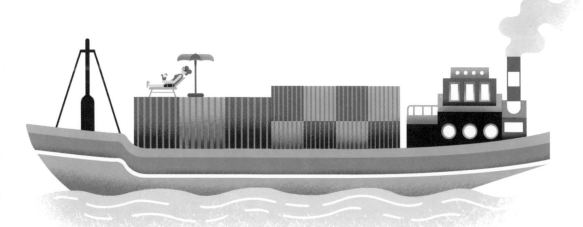

THE TRUTH ABOUT FLIGHT UPGRADES
How to maximise your chances of getting that mythical upgrade to first class

Getting an upgrade to a superior cabin on a flight is a bit like getting rid of hiccups – there are dozens of colourful theories for doing it, but no foolproof solution. In truth, the only trick isn't really a trick: you've got to work on your status.

'In the event of cabins being overbooked the decision is in the hands of the gate crew,' says Tom Otley, Editorial Director at Business Traveller. 'They can see the details of the tickets you've booked, and how many loyalty points you have. If you're a regular traveller, and have higher status than other passengers on that flight, then you get the bump up.'

That, then, is the unromantic truth. There remains, of course, no harm in flashing those baby blues at check-in. Where there's a spare seat in F there's always a chance.

Take the bump

Getting upgraded is a perk, but a more lucrative tweak to your journey is being bumped off an overbooked flight – often in exchange for vouchers, tier points or cash. If you're waiting to board and hear offers of compensation to those willing to take the bump, position yourself by the desk so you're best placed to swoop and grab the goodies.

ONLINE HOTEL BOOKING SUGGESTIONS

Tricks of the trade for finding the right accommodation – and at the right price

Book early

Hotel rooms are released on to the market 18 months in advance. In general the earlier you book the better as this is when prices are lower.

Book a flight and hotel together

If you are booking a flight and the hotel, not only will you benefit from lower flight prices earlier, but hotels also offer great value deals for advanced bookings and you can save by booking the two together. Booking flights+hotel also offers added consumer protection under EU package law.

Look for features, not stars

You may think you need a four star, but if it's just because you want a treadmill and free wifi, you might even find a hostel or apartment that offers this for a lot less.

Avoid peak times

Friday and Saturday are often more expensive than other days for most hotels, but if you are booking a hotel in a business district it may be easier to find cheaper deals at the weekend.

With thanks to Expedia (www.expedia.com) for suggestions.

WORLD RAIL TRAVEL FAQ
An expert's advice on seeing the world by train

How can I get the best deals on InterRail?

Using an InterRail pass can save you money, especially if you're under 26, want flexible travel dates, and/or you intend to clock up a fair old mileage. Do be aware that many trains charge a passholder reservation fee. Passholder places are limited by a quota on some routes, notably those to, from and within France.

Is my stuff safe?

Stories of audacious acts of theft on trains are as old as railways themselves so take other travellers' tales with a pinch of salt. What threat there is comes from outside the train.

What about food?

Don't assume there's a restaurant car, or that you'll want to eat anything from it. Bring snacks, and enough to share – trains are sociable places the world over.

How far ahead of travel are tickets released?	
United States	11 months
Canada	11 months
Australia	11 months
UK	12 weeks
Most of western Europe	90–92 days
Most of eastern Europe	60 days
India	60 days
Russia and Ukraine	45 days

Mark Smith, founder of train travel site Seat61.com

HOW TO GET THE BEST DEAL ON A HOTEL ROOM

Hotel prices are so much more transparent these days – online comparison sites do the haggling for you – but there are still some things you can do yourself

1 Many hotels, especially private ones, still work on a block-booking system for tour groups, holding allocations that may be unconfirmed. The magic hour is 6pm, when many hotels will re-release rooms that haven't been taken. Someone else's no-show can work to your advantage.

2 Look out for advance-purchase rates. These are often available 21 or 28 days in advance, but conditions can be quite strict.

3 An empty hotel room is one of the most perishable items on the planet. The hotelier has one night to sell it and then that night is gone forever so the later it gets, the more chance you have of twisting someone's arm: your something is better than their nothing.

4 Arriving late may not be the worst thing in the world, especially if you phone ahead to confirm you're coming. As rooms fill up you might find yourself upgraded to a better room.

Robert Dee, Sales Director for the Rezidor Hotel Group, operators of the Radisson Blu and Park Inn brands

ULTIMATE TRAVEL GADGETS
Techy kit that will turbo-charge your trip

- -

As part of the research for this book we asked a host of experts to recommend their essential bits of kit they couldn't travel without. Some things came up again and again...

>> **Tablet + USB keyboard** = a computer that can be carried lightly and used anywhere

>> **World plug adaptor** with multiple USB ports – the power junkie's dream come true. In seconds, every drained gizmo can be recharged

>> **Noise-cancelling headphones** – perfect for those very, very noisy bus journeys

>> **Portable source of power**, such as those make by powertraveller (powertraveller.com), to make your equipment batteries go further

>> **Travel hair-dryer** and **iron** – small, folding, light, and the best ones offer a variety of voltage

>> Compact **travel binoculars**. Not sure if you need them? Try them for one trip, and see how popular you become as well as how much more you see

>> Something to stand your camera or phone up while you take a steadier shot like the **Gorilla Pod** (joby.com/gorillapod)

CHOOSE YOUR
GADGET

FIRST-TIMERS TIPS FOR PRIVATE LODGINGS

Tips on renting an apartment, spare room, sofa – or even a garden – by the night

The world of accommodation has got a lot bigger with advent of online (and mobile) booking services for privately owned spaces. For first-timers the choice can be bewildering.

Andy Murdock, Managing Editor at Airbnb, explains that the key is remembering that the host is inviting you into their home. 'Trust is all-important. Have a proper profile on the site that shows who you are.' He adds, 'Just because a calendar is open, it doesn't necessarily mean it is open to you.' The host will want to check you out and be confident you're a good egg before accepting your booking.

Murdock also recommends opening up a dialogue before booking. 'If you think a place may be suitable, ask any questions you need. This back-and-forth is a key way of building confidence on both sides.'

Pay close attention to which part of town you're in. 'By nature of staying in someone's home you'll usually be a journey away from the main tourist sights. So choose your neighbourhood with care.'

Hedge your bets

Send multiple booking requests simultaneously – that way you have a chance to compare but also can be relatively sure that one will accept you.

WHAT YOU NEED TO KNOW ABOUT GROUND TRANSPORT

Tips for making those gruelling land journeys a little more inviting

Be organised

Book ahead for ground transport if at all possible – everything from first-class rail to budget buses rewards those who can plan in advance. Sometimes the fare can be low enough to mean that if you end up not taking this route at this time it's not the end of the world.

Freshen up

Pack a complete change of clothes on long-distance train and bus services. Even with a few minutes in a station, if you can whip out a bag with one clean set of everything and dash to the toilet you'll return to your journey feeling a little less like you've been on it for as long as you have.

Check for local holidays

Ground transport can become impractical or even impossible at public holiday time, depending on where you are in the world. This is a good time to book in somewhere interesting for a few days and nose around town, taking in any celebrations or seeing quiet corners.

Get on your bike

Investigate cheap, convenient bike-hire schemes, like the Paris Velib (www.velib.paris.fr). An increasing number of cities lay on these no-nonsense clunkers for locals and visitors, and they can be a tremendous alternative to a long walk or sweaty public-transport journey.

TRAVEL MONEY READY RECKONER

Don't be caught out by hidden fees or ballooning budgets – pick the right money option for you

Method of carrying money	Pros	Cons	Top tip
Cash	Cash remains convenient, and the risk of fraud is low	Risk of theft – once cash is gone, you won't get it back	Order cash online in advance to get better rates than high street or airports
Debit card	Keeps expenditure limited to your usual bank account, so can easily keep track of your spendings	Risk of being locked out of your account: tell your bank you're travelling. Also, watch the fees you're paying	If asked if you want to pay in your own currency, don't: you'll usually get an unfavourable exchange rate
Credit card	Ease of use: ATMs worldwide will accept your card	Two fees: an exchange charge and a loading fee per transaction. These vary hugely between cards	Shop around for cards offering reduced or no withdrawal fees on overseas transactions. The differences can be vast
Prepaid currency card	Transfer money online and use like you would a credit or debit card	Fees: compare setup, ATM withdrawal and, in particular, any inactivity charges	Limit the number of cash withdrawals to get the best value from these cards
Traveller's Cheques	Still seen as a safe option due to ease of reissue	Value: with declining use, exchange rates offered have declined considerably	For some destinations value may be better. If you're a TC loyalist, shop around

HOW TO FIND OUT IF A HOTEL IS AS GREEN AS IT'S MAKING OUT

Find a bone fide eco-resort for peace of mind

Heating, lighting and air-con consumption

Good eco-hotels use off-grid energy (like solar panels and wind turbines), thick insulation (eg double-glazing), low energy light bulbs and master keycards that control the room's electricity, aircon and heating.

Avoiding water waste

A sure sign that a hotel limits water usage is if it uses flow-restrictors in its taps and showerheads, and has installed dual flush toilets. Keep an eye out for refillable pump dispensers in the bathroom instead of wasteful packets of plastic miniatures.

Your food's air miles

Check the hotel's menu to see if it grows its own fruit and vegetables, and/or sources products from nearby suppliers. Look out for local, organic, seasonal food.

Get on your bike

The most progressive hotels encourage use of low emissions transport; for example, they provide a collection/drop-off service from nearby train or bus stations, and/or provide bikes for guests to use. Some hotels now provide charging points for electric cars and offer a discount if you arrive by electric car or public transport.

Richard Hammond, founder greentraveller.co.uk

THE VISA RUNNER'S HANDBOOK
How to get that stamp with minimum stress and fuss

Electronic visas and border-free areas like the European Union have taken some of the romance out of border crossings, but in many parts of the world you still need to sort visas in advance, or mount visa renewal runs across frontiers.

How can the intrepid traveller be prepared?

Matt Phillips, Lonely Planet's Destination Editor for Africa and veteran of many hot and bothered days chasing visas across the continent, says it can be a matter of preparation and patience. 'Travel armed with passport photos and a variety of denomination of US dollars. There can be lots of paperwork, and fees to pay, and then waiting around or repeated trips to the embassy.' Phillips recommends seeking out travellers coming the other way for advice and tips. 'If you can't find anyone, try the Thorn Tree (lonelyplanet.com/thorntree) – travellers often share experiences here.'

And if things aren't going your way?

'Keeping your cool will ensure a smoother experience. If you make an enemy of the person issuing the visa you may miss out – and it may not be their fault, either. Smile, persist, but have a back-up plan if things still look hopeless after a week.'

With any luck you'll have not only free passage to your destination of choice but a colourful passport stamp as a souvenir.

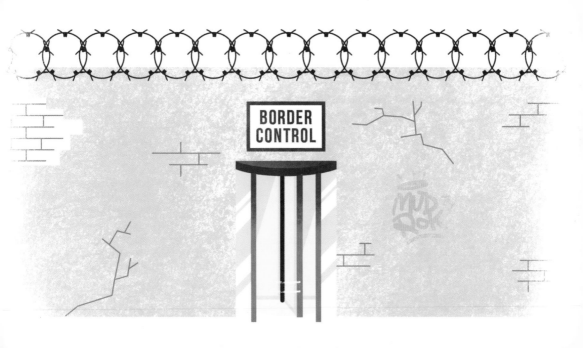

THE SECRET TO KEEPING TRACK OF YOUR MONEY
Fix yourself a realistic daily travel budget to avoid the bank manager's wrath on your return

Whether you're touring boutique boltholes or backpacking, here's how to make and not break a budgeting plan:

» Work out before you go how much you think you'll spend, then add a little for the first few days. More costs are incurred at the start of a trip as you get your bearings and settle in.

» Use available technology: online banking, SMS alerts and apps like Trail Wallet all help you keep a close eye on expenditure.

» Try a pre-loaded cash card like FairFX (see also page 42 on travel money). With one you can only spend what you have.

» Look for chances to save money but still get great experiences. Lunch can be a great time to eat out and take advantage of the better-value set menu deals. In the evening happy hours are also worth looking out for. But...

» Consider limiting alcohol – not only will daily boozing add up over even a two-week trip, but when you've had a few you're also more likely to lose control of what you're spending and throw caution to the wind.

Kash Bhattacharya, The Budget Traveller (budgettraveller.org)

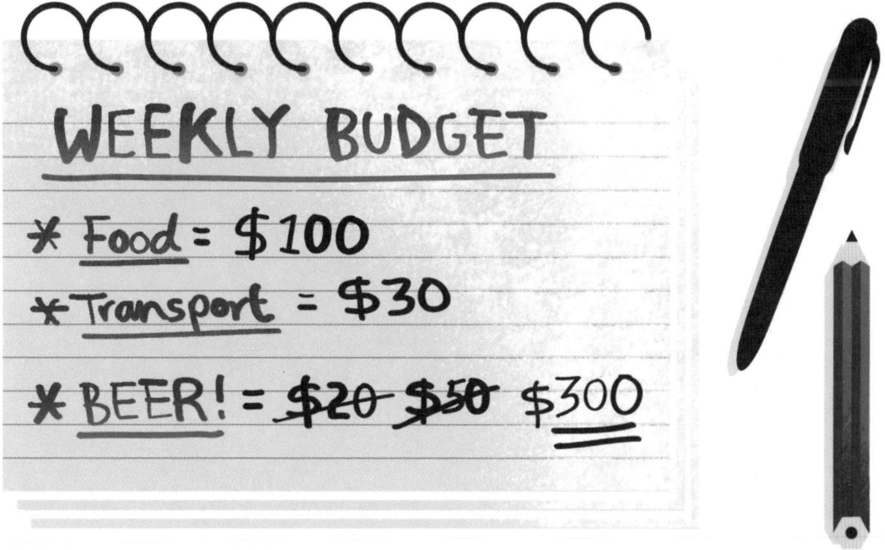
WEEKLY BUDGET
* Food = $100
* Transport = $30
* BEER! = ~~$20~~ ~~$50~~ $300

HOW TO BE A FLAWLESS TIPPER
Executing the correct tipping custom in a new country can be an etiquette minefield

1 Follow the local lead on tipping. If no one does, then don't. If tipping requires paying more on top than you would at home then not doing so might put you in an awkward position.

2 Being an overly generous tipper can have unintended consequences, especially for travellers who come after you. They may be expected to follow your lead.

3 Have a stash of low-denomination bills ready for doormen, porters and taxi drivers. Think of it as being part of the price, rather than an optional extra.

4 Seek out an independent source of truth for how much to tip and where. If someone has no vested interest in advising you to tip then you're more likely to get accurate information.

Turn to page 114 for a chart with accepted tipping rates of countries around the globe.

Tony Wheeler on tipping

When it comes to tipping it often pays to be suspicious about what's on your bill. If you can't speak about, or even read, what's on the bill then you don't know what's included. Seek out advice from hotel staff about what's commonly loaded on a bill.

OLD SCHOOL ITEMS
NO TRAVELLER SHOULD BE WITHOUT

Hi-tech gadgets aside, spare some space for old-school essentials that you never knew you needed

Sarah Baxter (Associate Editor at Wanderlust & travel writer, sarah-baxter.com) swears by the Casio F91-W watch. 'For $20 you get a watch that works for ages, has an alarm clock and simple light and, as it looks like it's straight out of 1981, will probably never be stolen. It's an absolute travel classic.'

Baxter also swears by packing a small bag containing safety pins, rubber bands and even an old pair of tights. Find room for a roll of duct tape too. Armed with these you can make on-the-go repairs, pin clothes and curtains and make a crude yet effective seal.

Don't assume you need high-tech clothing. 'You just need to be comfortable and wearing something quick-drying, unless you're doing something specialist like rock climbing or hardcore jungle trekking. Save your money for when you're on the road and need it.'

Poste Restante lives!

One of the great thrills of travel, especially long journeys, used to be picking up a pile of post from home. Despite the growth of the internet Poste Restante (French for post remaining) remains an international system for remote collection of post. This can be done in most locations worldwide, even small ones. In many cases you'll be picking up your mail from grand central post offices, though for the most fun try getting mailed in obscure locations.

BEATING THE HOTEL CHECK-IN RULES
There's no need to be that sorry-looking scruffpot waiting in reception for hours

The dreaded mid-afternoon check-in has made many a journey to get to a meeting or wedding stressful, with the prospect of nowhere to drop your bags, get changed or freshen up.

Forty winks

If you're after a nap, seek out the increasing number of capsule or cabin hotels at airports aimed at transitting travellers such as Yotel (www.Yotel.com) for a few hours' extra sleep. You can also, in some airports, have a shower on arrival.

Start by calling the hotel before making a booking and explaining the situation. As you're a paying guest they should want you to be happy, and should at least try to help. Ask to have a note put on the system requesting an early check-in.

If you don't manage to get in your room, ask your hotel to store your bags. You can either wait it out or try to find somewhere for a shower: swimming pools and train stations are good places to try. Leave your phone number with the hotel and ask them to call when your room is available.

CLAW BACK THE COST OF YOUR TRIP
Take the chance to reclaim those all-important pennies

The silver lining on that missed flight
You may not be able to get a refund on that budget airline flight, but you can reclaim the tax on any portion of a journey you haven't taken.

Recoup on purchase made abroad
Depending on where you are you can usually claim back certain taxes paid on purchases made while travelling. Check out the regulations for where you're going and where you've been, as there will be forms to fill in (that you can usually pick up at point of purchase). Payment for services such as hotels and car hire cannot generally be claimed back.

Know the inside track
As odd as it sounds, check if certain elements of your holiday are tax-deductible, as they may be if, for instance, you combine a holiday with a business trip. Your home government should have advice online.

Don't lose out on leftover currency
While the exchange rate for repatriating your left-over holiday funds into your own currency will be poor at departure points, you can often find zero-commission fees back at your point of purchase. Or at larger hostels you may be able to strike a deal with a fellow traveller - if legal to do so of course.

BEAT JETLAG!
Just why do we feel in such bad shape at the end of a long journey?

Any long journey can be stressful and exhausting, with sleep loss, physical discomfort and disruption of eating/drinking patterns. The key point about planning a long haul journey is to keep these factors to a minimum, and to travel with as much comfort, convenience and lack of disruption as is practical or affordable: sometimes it is very hard to achieve the right balance!

Then there's the impact of crossing time zones rapidly, which causes fatigue and sleep disruption in an entirely different way. Correctly timed exposure to daylight or bright light can help you adjust faster to your new time zone. Melatonin has also been shown to help, with a small dose taken at bedtime.

It's perfectly reasonable to talk to your doctor about using short-acting sleeping pills to reduce sleep loss: you can use them to initiate sleep at a normal bedtime, after a long journey from west to east; or to help you get back to sleep in the middle of the night after travels from east to west. There are also newer prescription medicines (such as modafinil) that can improve alertness and travellers through the worst effects. Medicines don't change the pace of adjustment to a new time zone, but will at least help reduce fatigue and sleep loss.

Dr Richard Dawood , Director of the Fleet Street Clinic, London

EAT WELL WHILE TRAVELLING
...and avoid a scale-bending welcome home

Pre-holiday diets are no fun at all, but how can you make sure that your holiday doesn't leave you with a souvenir round your waist that makes the homecoming blues especially painful?

》 Think about what you're eating. Like at home, steamed or boiled beats fried. Keep up the five a day and swap in fruit – washed in clean water – for sugary snacks. Choosing the occasional granita rather than gelato will help too.

》 A tip practised by power-lunching business travellers is to order two starters instead of a starter and a main. Tapas-style small plates is a good way to try lots of things without necessarily scoffing half of Spain.

》 Self-catering for one meal a day is a good idea even on smaller trips. You're less likely to splurge if cooking for yourself. Visiting a local market to stock up is lots of fun too.

》 Your travelling companion is your ally on your quest to eat well, and healthily. You can share portions, cutting costs and calories while still having a meal out.

》 Don't deny yourself too much but keep an eye on things – tightening clothes are the tell-tale sign that your round-the-world odyssey may be making you slightly too, umm, round.

Liz Edwards, food and travel writer and editor

HOW TO BE A WOMAN TRAVELLING ALONE

... and enjoy your trip even more as a result

The idea of going it alone on a big trip is daunting for anyone and perhaps more so for women, for whom safety issues can be more of a concern. Don't let this put you off. Travelling as a solo woman opens up a whole world of new experiences as you learn to navigate situations on your own, forge unusual friendships and basically do whatever you want whenever you want. Empowering as it might be, however, it's worth bearing the following tips in mind to ensure your trip goes smoothly.

1 Plan ahead, so you know what you should be wearing, so you avoid arriving in a new place late at night, so you always have enough money on you, and so on.

2 Read up on what is culturally acceptable and what is not. This way you avoid drawing attention to yourself for all the wrong reasons.

3 Having done your reading, trust your instinct: if you are comfortable you know what's happening, nothing beats female instinct for keeping you safe.

4 Know why you have decided to travel alone and be happy with that decision as this will help you with the many hundreds of decisions you'll make on your trip, from where you go to who you decide to engage with. And take that positive mindset with you: it will open so many doors.

Imogen Hall

EXPERT'S GUIDE TO AVOIDING THEFT AND SCAMS
Thieves prey on the unsuspecting – so get clued up to stay safe

Firstly, adopt an anti-scam mindset in everyday life so it's second nature when travelling. For instance, don't let your credit card out of sight in restaurants and be cautious revealing personal information. This means you don't have to adjust your behaviour on the road.

Once travelling, one of the best ways to avoid being targeted is to blend in as much as possible: wear clothes worn in the region (that is, no shorts and Hawaiian shirts in Paris), don't walk around with a camera on show and avoid opening maps – duck into a cafe to read them discretely, or buy a local street directory.

Learning a phrase in the local language such as 'Saya tinggal di Bali' – 'I live in Bali' (or the equivalent for whichever destination) has an amazing effect on dispelling nefarious types.

Have a hand/carry bag with interior pockets, so your wallet can't easily be lifted, even if people manage to reach into your bag. Wearing your bag across your body also stops it being easy to swipe.

Catherine Le Nevez, Lonely Planet author and travel writer

SCAMS TO WATCH OUT FOR
Repeat the matra: it's too good to be true, it's too good to be true...

While you're often safer overseas than you are in your home town, a few scams seem to pop up all over the world.

The scam: fake police Sometimes also real police, they'll demand to see your passport, find something wrong with your visa but suggest your troubles will be over if you pay a fine. To them. In cash. Right now.
What to do Standing your ground and offering to accompany them to the station will usually see the error 'excused'.

The scam: gem or carpet deals On entry into a store, often prompted by an enthusiastic taxi or rickshaw driver, you will be offered a deal so preposterously lucrative that refusing seems unthinkable.
What to do Think again – those gems are going to be worthless and the carpet you buy may not make it home at all. There are legitimate traders selling both jewels and rugs, and they don't act like this.

Bird poo The surprising splat of birdshit landing on you from a great height is followed by the swift appearance of a stranger who towels you down. In the confusion, valuables are removed from your person, never to be seen again.
What to do Move fast. If you seem to have been to have been the victim of a bird strike, keep moving and avoid any offers of help.

BIG FOOT SAFARI
Cheap GEMS
FREE Tours
FREE HOTEL
$$$
UNICORN NEST

AVOIDING PITFALLS

THINGS NOT TO USE WHEN TRAVELLING
Don't fall for overpriced services – stay smart and save cash

It pays to know what is and isn't worth bothering with while travelling. If you come up against a stiff charge there's usually an affordable alternative within easy reach. Many of these charges can be found in your hotel room - I'm waiting for the day hotels charge you just for looking in the minibar. Or even thinking about it.

What not to use	Suggested alternative
Hotel internet	Coffee shop wifi
Hotel minibar	A drink at the bar round the corner
Hotel laundry	A Sunday afternoon at a local Laundromat
Data roaming on your phone	Locally-purchased SIM card
Taxis (without the meter turned on)	Pre-booked taxis
Bureau de Change at airports	Pre-booked online currency exchange
Any phone to make international calls	Skype or Google Hangout

Tony Wheeler, co-founder, Lonely Planet

BUREAU DE CHANGE

Mini Bar

DUTY-FREE Jewellery

DO NOT CROSS

DO NOT CROSS

DO NOT CROSS

DO NOT CROSS

DO NOT CROSS

DO NOT CROSS

ALWAYS BE HEALTHY WHILE TRAVELLING

Sometimes mishaps are inevitable – but there are simple ways to reduce the risk of sickness and injury when on the road

Avoid bites

Whenever and wherever you travel in the tropics, cover up, use lots of insect repellent, and protect yourself from bites during the night using plug-ins, mosquito coils and/or a mosquito net.

Don't expect to avoid common complaints

Pack a medical kit to help you cope with common ailments like cold, flu, headaches, allergies and indigestion, not just with tropical ailments in mind.

Remember risks

Remember that enjoying the nightlife, sports, swimming, cycling, diving, and using a moped or motorbike may be more dangerous than at home, and the medical care poorer. Prevention is everything!

Wash your hands!

Wherever and whatever you eat, always make sure that your hands are clean – carry a small bottle of hand sanitizer to use before handling food.

Stay in touch

There's a big choice of medical guides to consult if problems arises. There are email or SMS-based systems that can send you alerts about new risks arising while you're on the road. And it is easier than ever to stay in touch with your own doctor or travel clinic if you need medical help while away.

Dr Richard Dawood, Director of the Fleet Street Clinic in London and author of *Travellers' Health: How to stay healthy abroad*

FITNESS HACKS FOR TRAVELLERS
When there's no time, no room or no gym for that big workout

Physio Katherine McNabb (bodyfixphysio.co.uk) suggests a few exercises to keep you trim and toned from hotel room or airport lounge.

Hip flexor stretch
》 Kneel on a towel on one knee, with the other leg in front, with the foot on the floor.
》 Squeeze your bottom muscles and gently push the back hip forward to stretch it.
》 Swap sides and repeat.

Bridging
》 Lie on the floor with your knees bent up.
》 Rest your hands on the front of the pelvis, then lift your bottom up and hold. Imagine a spirit level staying perfectly balanced across your stomach.

》 If this is easy, lift one leg straight in front whilst holding your bottom off the floor. The trick is not to wobble or twist the pelvis.
》 Hold for 10 seconds, then repeat on the other side.

Superman (aka Table Top)
》 Get on your hands and knees with your hips over your knees and your shoulders over your hands – just like a table.
》 Slowly lift one leg out straight behind you and lift the opposite arm out in front. Try not to wobble or twist your back, and make sure your face looks at the floor so your neck is straight.
》 Hold for 10 seconds, then repeat on the other side.

WHEN TO CHOW DOWN ON STREET FOOD
... and when to pass

Choose your time of day
Markets tend to swing into action early, so be prepared to have breakfast rather than lunch. If somewhere is busy at five or six in the morning it's a good indicator of quality.

Get close to the source
Ceviche in Lima or sushi in Tokyo is more likely to be the real deal. Non-western approximations of western food, such as hamburgers, involve some second-guessing.

Shop around
Don't go for the first places you see. These are most likely the ones that get most tourist traffic and offer the least authentic experience. They might feel more accessible, but locals probably won't go here.

Trust your nose, not your eyes
In food markets the emphasis is on the produce, not the aesthetics of presentation. This stretches to the food made to be eaten on the premises.

Join the queue
Popularity is a good indicator of quality so if there's a queue maybe you should join it.

Luke Waterson, food and travel writer
(englishmaninslovakia.com)

CLASSIC HONEYMOON FAILS
– AND HOW TO AVOID THEM
Make sure your first trip as a married couple is as perfect as you've planned

That beautiful beach. Just you and your newly betrothed. Bliss, right? Hopefully. But honeymoons are surprisingly easy to get wrong. Here's how to get off to a long life together on the right track.

Plan together
It's tempting for one of you to take on planning the honeymoon while the other books the band and caterer. Plan together and you're more likely to get what you both want from the trip.

Beach blues
Organising a wedding can be stressful. While the idea of flopping on a beach might appeal, it may prove harder to switch off than if you start with something urban or active for a few days to wind down.

> **Get inspired**
> See www.101honeymoons.co.uk for all manner of honeymoon ideas.

Go for your dream honeymoon
If you've always dreamed of lemur-spotting in Madagascar or kayaking in Alaska together then you've got the perfect excuse to go. Just because the beach break is the stereotypical honeymoon doesn't mean it is right for you and your beloved.

Travel as a gift
Friends love to contribute to your honeymoon in lieu of a toaster or set of teaspoons that you already have. Many travel companies offer wedding lists that make great, alternative gifts.

35

COMPLAIN WELL
Ingrid Stone, author of *Letters of a Dissatisfied Woman*
(lettersofadissatisfiedwoman.com) on the fine art of complaining

Don't be shy
Don't forget you've paid a lot of money for your flight, experience or hotel room. If something's not right, speak up. Travellers are great at moaning, but not so good at raising complaints.

Speak up early
Travel firms want to deal with problems promptly. If something's not right, say so then. When it's raised later, it can be harder to make amends.

Get social
Customer service departments now monitor social networks, Twitter in particular, and are quick to respond to problems. Sign up before you go and follow the relevant accounts to speed things up.

EU Airline compensation rules
Flying to or from the EU? It pays to know your rights as you could entitled to compensation in the event of delays or cancellation. See the EU website for more details.

Keep calm and carry on
Being angry is not the right way, no matter what the issue. Be polite, but firm. You'll be taken more seriously if you don't act like a ranting maniac.

Consider writing a letter
A well-written letter, especially one showing a sense of humour, gives you room to make a point and will have a big impact if it gets in front of the right people. Keep copies of all correspondence.

DON'T BE LEFT POWERLESS
Keep your devices humming as you travel along the open road

Power, in the form of fuel for your phone, tablet or digital camera, is almost as high on the modern traveller's hierarchy of needs as food and water. Here's how to find the fuel you need.

Only use what you need
The more apps it's running, the faster your smartphone will drain. Switch off what you aren't using – including 3G or 4G – and you'll keep things going for longer.

Go offline
Offline maps and other downloadable apps can save you having to be online the whole time – another big drainer of power, not to mention cost.

Look for different sources of power
As well as portable, rechargeable batteries, look for plug adaptors with multiple USB connections, and remember you can use your laptop to charge many devices. Some laptops will even charge out once they themselves have powered off, via a still-active USB port.

Keep your hotel room's charge flowing
Many hotel room plugs aren't active when the key to turn on the lights and other appliances is removed. In some hotels you can hack this by placing any credit-card sized object in the slot, allowing you to charge while you're out and about.

Shawn Low, travel writer

HOW TO TURN RAINY SEASONS TO YOUR ADVANTAGE

Have a great trip, avoid the crowds of the dry season – and even get a tan

Common wisdom holds you shouldn't travel in the rainy season. Clearly, it will be wet, and who wants a soggy holiday? But before switching plans, it pays to look a little closer. Thailand's rains, for instance, often come at night and leave quiet beaches and blue skies by day.

Chris McIntyre, Managing Director of Expert Africa (www.expertafrica.com) advises, 'Come in the dry, and you'll see animals around waterholes, but vegetation is sparse and there's not much going on. Come when the rains start and you'll experience everything coming to life, which is truly magical.' Of course, some sights,

like waterfalls, are at their most dramatic during the wet season.

Cost is also a good reason to travel at monsoon time. Temporary camps may close, but those that stay open can offer terrific value. The lower demand can also mean that what would be peak season elsewhere, like July and August in India, is an affordable – if hot and sticky – time to travel.

The secret is to look very closely at your destination's weather patterns – microclimates can change things from one region to the next – and speak to locals and travellers who've been before you.

38 AVOID OFFENCE, ALWAYS
How to stay on everyone's right side as you travel

It's fairly difficult to cause so much offence as to get you into trouble. Generally people you meet will be tolerant and understanding. The exceptions are offending local religious sensibilities, especially in stricter Islamic countries, and voicing unpopular views about the government or royal family of the country you're in.

Do:
>> Learn some local phrases, including 'excuse me' and 'I'm sorry' and air them when you need to.
>> Follow the lead of those around you: if others are removing shoes or donning headscarves, do the same.
>> Smile! You'll find far more people ready to forgive the foibles of a visitor than those who take permanent offence.

Don't:
>> Emulate your fellow tourists' bad habits – scribbling your name on ancient monuments is not cool.
>> Take what might appear to be a local litter problem as an excuse to drop your own trash.
>> Take pictures at sensitive military, religious or political spots, including demonstrations.

DEVELOP YOUR PHOTO-TAKING ROUTINE
Learn the art of snap-happy to achieve the best shots

Potential images abound – they will come and go in front of your eyes in a matter of seconds and are easily missed. A good routine plays a big part in helping you find great subjects and react quickly enough to capture them.

>> Get out and walk. You'll add first-hand knowledge to your research, and the map will make more sense.
>> Get up early. The light is often at its best, the activity in towns is at its most intense and interesting. You'll be rewarded with experiences and images that most people miss.
>> Have your camera around your neck, switched on and with the lens cap off. And fit the lens you're most likely to need.

Show off your wares
The weekly Lonely Planet Flickr photo competition is a great place to showcase your work among a travel-mad photography community. Check it out at www.flickr.com/groups/lonelyplanetpublications

>> Be aware of existing light conditions and have your camera set accordingly. Constantly check the ISO setting, especially if you're in and out of low-light interiors.
>> If a subject appeals, never assume that you'll see it again later.

By Richard I'Anson, double Master of Photography and author of *Lonely Planet's Best Ever Photography Tips*

WHEN TABLET BEATS BOOK AND WHEN BOOK BEATS TABLET

Ebooks or paper books the choice is yours

In the book corner

In the tablet corner

Books don't have a limited battery life. If you're using a paper guidebook, you can spend time getting the information you want and getting out, not searching for a wall point or Wi-Fi

Books are bulky, get in the way of your other stuff, and can be heavy. Digital chapters of guides don't weigh anything and can be downloaded from anywhere

If lost, a tablet will be expensive to replace. You'll also incur costs buying and insuring one

A tablet can carry hundreds of books, magazines and movies

You can always borrow a guide if you need to look something up, or swap books with other travellers when you finish them

By syncing your tablet with other devices you can always switch from one to another

Books don't like rain, or falling off the side of a canoe, but will survive both: paper floats

You can always film your book bobbing off the side of a canoe on your tablet

TOP TIPS ON TANTRUM-FREE HOLIDAYS WITH KIDS

Family trips can be a testing time, so it pays to do your planning in advance

Know your audience

Choose somewhere age appropriate for your kids. It's no good forcing toddlers to do city tours when all they want to do is hang out by the pool or beach.

The great outdoors

If you're on a tight budget – or even if you're not – never underestimate how much kids love camping.

Sweeten them up

Facing a tough flight with a toddler? Worried about how your fellow passengers will react? Bribe them. A few candies break the ice and mean that your neighbour has an incentive not to tut or sigh (too loudly).

Flying high

If you're facing a significant time difference on arrival, it could be worth adjusting your kids' bedtimes slightly before you go to ease the transition.

Get involved

Kids will always get more out of their trip if you engage them with local culture and food. It's great to take along a booklet for them to create a holiday diary. Even for kids that don't enjoy writing, they can fill the diary with train tickets, postcards, drawings – anything to remind them of the destination once home. They will also get extra points from their teachers when they return to school!

Jane Anderson, familytraveller.com

42

FUN
FACTOR

SECRETS ONLY SOLO TRAVELLERS KNOW
...and why everyone should have a go at travelling alone

》 Solo travellers get more breaks. More often than not it's easier to squeeze one extra person on a trip, or fill a spare seat, or even grab that upgrade (see page 28). Just one more person doesn't tip the scales like a couple or group.

》 On your own you're better at joining in, and you're never outnumbering or intimidating if approaching others. Leave the headphones off for extra approachable points.

》 While the perception is that solo travellers are more vulnerable, often the opposite is true. You're reliant on your own gut instinct, without peer pressure.

》 You're rarely on your own when travelling on your own. You make friends faster and have the freedom to change plans to spend more time with those you do get on with. And if not? There's nothing keeping you in town when you feel like moving on.

Matt Phillips, Destination Editor at Lonely Planet

CAPTURE THE TRIP

Don't limit yourself to photos– collect tangible reminders of your holiday for your shelves or scrapbook

Some unusual things to take home that will bring back the memory of your trip in years to come...

》 Ticket stubs from public transport

》 Fallen leaves

》 A CD by a popular local band

》 Beer bottle label

》 Postcards sent to yourself from the road

》 Shirt of national sports team or, if that's too expensive, shorts or socks

》 Well-thumbed guidebook

》 A map of the city or country you've been with your route sketched on it

》 Sound recording of street scenes

》 Army surplus (cheap and easy to find at markets)

》 A musical instrument

》 Your own sketches drawn while travelling

Seb Neylan, Social Media Manager at Lonely Planet

ACE YOUR SMALL GROUP ADVENTURE
Joining a group can be a great way to explore a country and make new friends

1 As well as getting a taste of a different culture, you will be spending lots of time with a group of new people – so it pays to do your homework. Different companies and types of tour will bring together people of different nationalities and ages, so check you're signing up for one that's right for you.

2 Being on time on your trip is more than a common courtesy to your guide and fellow group members. It might be the difference between making an early morning bus or catching the greatest sunset of your life. Nothing will erode goodwill faster than missing agreed departure times.

3 Use the guide for local knowledge – they are there to do more than get you from a to b. They can help you get a good price on souvenirs, recommend a great bar for after-hours revelry or get you tickets for the big match in town.

4 Read the itinerary beforehand and check there's enough free time. With a little wiggle room you can make time for solo jaunts as well as enjoying the pre-arranged plan.

5 Steer clear of controversial topics such as religion or politics when enjoying communal conversations, especially when alcohol is involved.

Casey Mead, G Adventures

45

FUN
FACTOR

TURN ANY BUSINESS TRIP INTO A MINI BREAK
Make the most of being somewhere new – even if you spend most of your time in an office

Use those jetlagged hours
Strolling in the early hours can be magical, and make you feel like you're the only traveller in town. Some things, like markets, are at their best very early. You could even aim for a celebrated cross-town coffee shop for breakfast, giving you a slice of local life before your colleagues are ready to get down to work.

Look at listings before you travel
Getting tickets for a show or sporting event can be easier than you think, and often impresses your hosts. A spare ticket for a baseball match or concert rarely goes begging.

Make the most of down-time
Even the busiest schedules include spare hours,

such as lunchtime or pre-dinner. Look into cycle-hire schemes that could allow you to whizz around and see something of the city.

Go for the big thing
One 'must-do' in the city? Make plans to see it with a colleague in advance of arriving. This can help to make it a more concrete part of your schedule when you might be tempted to drop it in favour of another working dinner.

> **Pro tip from Tom Otley, Editorial Director at Business Traveller**
>
> Pack your trainers: many larger hotels offer jogging maps with pre-planned routes around parks, traffic-free paths and even landmarks.

SOCIAL MEDIA FOR TRAVELLERS
How to make social sites and apps work for you

It's easy to waste time on social media when travelling: by the time you read this, selfies in front of the seven wonders of the modern world should be officially declared uncool. But some social media has a genuine utility beyond posting tagged pictures from wherever you are.

》 Store your images on the go using **Flickr**. If you don't want to share with the world you can make your photos private or only share with friends. There's an handy auto-upload app for smartphones so you don't have to do it manually.

》 **Twitter** is an excellent way to access customer service teams. (See p. 78 for how to use Twitter to your advantage when complaining.)

》 Find your friends, see where's popular and get promotions and deals from businesses on **Foursquare**.

》 Keep track of your trip using **Instagram**. Geotagged photos can add up to a great souvenir of any trip and over time the world map becomes a visual record of all your travels.

》 Lastly, **Foodspotting** is great for gastronomes and fussy eaters alike, allowing you to slaver over pictures of the food you'll find wherever you're heading next.

Emma Sparks, travel blogger and Social Media Coordinator at Lonely Planet

HOW A CONCIERGE CAN MAKE YOUR TRIP UNSTOPPABLE
Think a concierge is only for wealthy business types? Think again

Jose Pacuo, Head Concierge at the Milestone Hotel, London (www.milestonehotel.com) offers some suggestions on when a concierge can make the difference to your trip.

A good concierge is the gatekeeper to their city, and is the key to unlocking exactly the experiences a guest at their hotel is after. So they're a great place to start for personalised suggestions and advice on tours and outings. As they're specialists in their city, you can expect a pretty accurate and tailored piece of advice.

Concierges are engaged by guests in a variety of ways – from helping with basic necessities like finding a parking space or getting directions to planning the entire duration of a stay. If you have an unusual request, like trying to source a particular item as a gift back home, a concierge can save you time and help you find the best in class, and even arrange to buy it for you.

An experienced concierge won't be fazed even by unusual requests, so don't be shy in asking for their help. If they don't know the answer themselves they'll have an impeccable contacts book to find someone in the city who does.

48

FUN FACTOR

ADVENTURE UP YOUR TRIP
Try a new approach to zing up your trip and throw up unexpected experiences

Destination not exciting enough for you? Adventurer and TV presenter Simon Reeve (simonreeve.co.uk) has some suggestions on how to add some spice to your vacation.

Go out at night, and dawn. Exploring a new locale shouldn't be restricted to 9 to 5, and there's always a surprise to be had watching a city after dark, or just as it's waking up.

Ditch the big sights: take pleasure in detail. Draw a circle around your home-base using a glass and explore the area forensically.

Pore over local press. Forget international news and CNN. Nothing will immerse you in where you are like local news. If all you find is mundanity then you can relish finding a rare, quiet part of the world.

The road less travelled

Latourex (The LABoratory of EXperimental TOURism; www.latourex.org) is a treasure-trove of way-out ways to shake up your travels.

Camp. In particular, wild camp. It heightens senses and brings you into closer contact with your surroundings.

Travel randomly. Flip a coin at intersections and follow your nose.

WHEN YOU CAN'T CONTROL THE WEATHER
A rainy day needn't be a wash-out

Sunshine destinations revolve around good weather, but cities pretty much keep going regardless. If the weather's ropey, consider making an urban excursion as a day trip from your holiday destination, and take advantage of museums and galleries.

Some outdoor activities (such as surfing) involve getting pretty wet anyway, so consider ways you can hit the beach even if things are inclement. A wetsuit will keep you warm for hours while messing around in the sea you should have pretty much to yourself.

Seek out local cinema and theatre – the smaller the better. This is not only a chance to mug up on local culture (try going to the cinema in India for a wildly different experience) but if you're lucky you'll discover a funky older building to boot.

For active pursuits like hiking there's no need to pause if the weather's bad, only to make sure you've the right gear. Consider packing a quick-drying travel towel if you're going somewhere it might be soggy.

Libraries can be an unusual but welcome refuge. Many now come with WiFi, and any decent one will have a stash of locally-themed books that can while away hours, immersing yourself in your destination.

**FUN
FACTOR**

THE ART OF BEING ZEN ON THE ROAD
... or how switching off devices can make your trip better

Looking at the world through a small screen? Constantly searching for Wi-Fi or a power point? Find yourself texting or Facebooking your way around the world? You may be missing out.

Travel writer Phillip Tang has some suggestions for kicking the technology habit while travelling. 'Make a conscious decision to leave devices behind, either at home or back in the hotel room. Without constant access to the web you're more reliant on local advice and word of mouth – both of which are instant, targetted and tailored to you.'

Ditching the devices has other desired effects too. 'Without the burden of something of value

you can wander more freely – down to the beach with just a towel, or to that part of town you weren't sure about venturing into,' says Tang.

And those people at home, tracking your trip and eager for updates? Make a regular time to catch up, on Skype or a Hangout, and stick to it. It'll make contact with home more of an event, and not eat into time you're spending discovering what's around you.

Phillip Tang, travel writer (philliptang.co.uk)

> Leave headphones off when moving around. It makes you more approachable and more aware of your surroundings.

QUICK-REFERENCE

TRAVEL HACKS

USEFUL APPS AND WEBSITES FOR TRAVELLERS

There's a plethora of brilliantly informative and helpful digital tools out there, to help you plan your trip and execute it flawlessly

Websites

Old school web 1.0 it may be, but the Universal Packing List, found at http://upl.codeq.info/, remains a fantastic tool.

Smart Packing (www.smartpacking.com) not only has printable packing tips for tourists, families and business travellers.

Money Saving Expert (www.moneysavingexpert.com) is a UK-based consumer champion website with huge amounts of information on holiday and flight booking, as well as general money-saving advice.

The websites of the US Consular Department (http://travel.state.gov), the UK Foreign & Commonwealth Office (www.fco.gov.uk) and the Australian Department of Foreign Affairs & Trade (www.dfat.gov.au) all offer up-to-date travel advice for the countries you're planning on visiting.

Reduce the risks of international road travel by getting information from the Association for Safe International Road Travel (www.asirt.org)

See AirSafe (www.airsafe.com) for facts and figures on air crashes, including tips on how to handle emergency situations.

Apps

Google Translate
Translate over 70 languages from speech or text

ByPost
Postcard creator and sender, using your images from on the road

TripIt
Invaluable travel organiser and itinerary planner

Gate Guru
Comprehensive airport information for terminals around the world

FlightStats
Live flight tracking and other stats

SpeedSpot
Gives the speed of internet connections and helps track down wifi spots around the world

WordLens
Uses your smartphones video camera to translate printed words

XE
Instant currency conversion

WORLD TIPPING CHART

Get up to speed with the tipping etiquette of your destination – customs vary the world over

Destination	Restaurants	Bars	Taxi Drivers
US	15%-20%	$1 a drink	10-15%
France	15% service charge by law, 5% optional	Rare	10%
Australia	5-10%	Change	Change
Thailand	Rounding up	Change	50-100B
New Zealand	5-10%	5-10%	round up to nearest dollar
UK	10-15%	Not expected	10% or round up to nearest pound
Spain	service charge by law optional 5-10%	No established rule	5% or rounding up
India	10-15% optional	Unusual to tip	Can tip honest drivers
Italy	10% optional	Small change	Uncommon
Egypt	12% service charge added, optional to add extra	No set amount, but it is expected.	

Destination	Restaurants	Bars	Taxi Drivers
Morocco	10%	10%	round up
Czech Republic	5-10%	5-10%	5-10%
Germany	5-10%	5%	5-10%
Turkey	10-15%		round up to n earest 50 kurus
Cuba	10%	1CUC per visit, not every drink	10%
Netherlands	up to 10%	up to 10%	round up/5%
Vietnam	5%	Not expected but appreciated	Not expected but appreciated
Canada	15%	10-15%	10-15%
Japan	Not customary	Not customary	Not customary
Ireland	10%	Uncommon	10%

GLOBAL CLIMATE MAP

Don't get caught out by the rainy seasons – pick your destination carefully to enjoy maximum sunshine

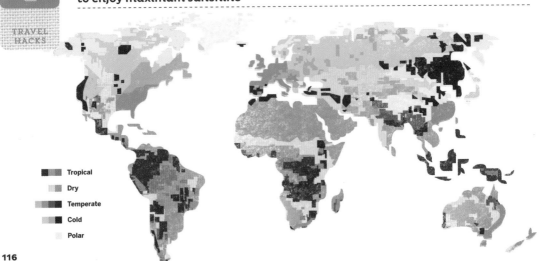

- Tropical
- Dry
- Temperate
- Cold
- Polar

MALARIA AROUND THE WORLD

It pays to know where in the world malaria can be transmitted. Learn more about staying safe from the mozzies on page 70.

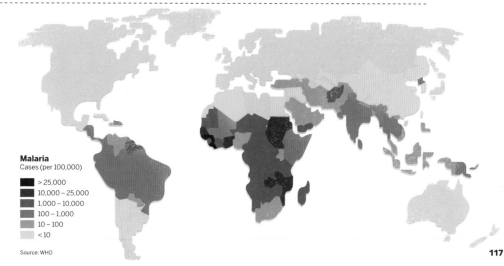

Malaria
Cases (per 100,000)

- > 25,000
- 10,000 – 25,000
- 1,000 – 10,000
- 100 – 1,000
- 10 – 100
- < 10

Source: WHO

YEAR-ROUND TRIP PLANNER

Whether you're craving adventure, culture or romance, we've got the world's best travel options covered, whatever the time of year

	January	February	March	April	May	June
Beach	East coast Australia	Gambia	Cape Verde	St Lucia	Crete	Sardinia
Active	Skiing in British Columbia	Yachting in the Whitsunday Islands, Australia	Trekking to Roraima, Venezuela	Rock-climbing in the Lake District, England	Snorkelling and scuba, Polynesia	Trekking the Andes, Peru
Culture	Temple-hopping in Thailand	Exploring Mughal Forts and Palaces, India	Colonial cities and music, Cuba	Vienna's Museums and Galleries, Austria	Old Kyoto, Japan	Art and architecture, Glasgow, Scotland
City	Prague	Cape Town	Beirut	Paris	Berlin	London
Honeymoon	Boutique Buenos Aires and luxury estancias, Argentina	Castaway beaches, Maldives	Partying in Rio, rainforest adventures, Brazil	Jamaica's quiet coves	Country house escape, England	Spa hideaway and diving, Bali & Lombok
Wildlife	Snakes & monkeys, Costa Rica	Whales and seals, Peninsular Valdes, Argentina	Orangutans, Borneo	Ningaloo Marine Park, Australia	Galapagos Islands, Ecuador	Wildebeest Migration, Kenya & Tanzania

	July	August	Sept	Oct	Nov	Dec
Beach	Ibiza, Spain	Cornwall, England	Fiji	Zanzibar, Tanzania	Florida Keys	Thailand
Active	Via Ferrrata, Italy	Cycling, Ireland	River Running the Grand Canyon, USA	Walking safari, Selous, Tanzania	Swim with Orcas, Tysfjord, Norway	Camel safari, Rajasthan
Culture	Classical concerts and Imperial treasure, St Petersburg, Russia	Silk Road cities, Uzbekistan	Ancient history and modern art, Istanbul, Turkey	Ancient and less ancient Rome, Italy	Morocco's Imperial Cities	Dancing and dining, Buenos Aires, Argentina
City	Reykjavik	Vancouver	Havana	New York	Auckland	Hong Kong
Honeymoon	Open-top cruising, Italy	Tropical retreat, Mauritius	Five-star Paris and chateaux, France	Cape Town and the Big Five, South Africa	Volcanoes and surf beaches, Hawaii	Once-in-a-lifetime Australia
Wildlife	Brown bears, Alaska	Gorillas, East Africa	Reindeer, Lapland	Cave glow-worms, New Zealand	Lemurs, Madagascar	Penguins, Antarctica

INTERNATIONAL PLUG SOCKETS

The world of plug sockets and adaptors can be a confusing place. Here's a rundown of some of the world's power fittings

Destination	Plug type	Compatible with others?
US	A, B	A
Canada	A, B	A
Thailand	O	-
Australia	I	-
New Zealand	I	-
UK and Ireland	G	-
Europe*	C, E, F	C, E, F
South Africa	M	-
China	I	-
Singapore	G	-
Malaysia	G	-
Japan	A, B	A
Brazil	N	C
India	D	C, D

* Except:

Switzerland and Lichtenstein
(type J, compatible with C)

Denmark
(type K, compatible with C)

Italy
(type L, compatible with C if socket is 10A)

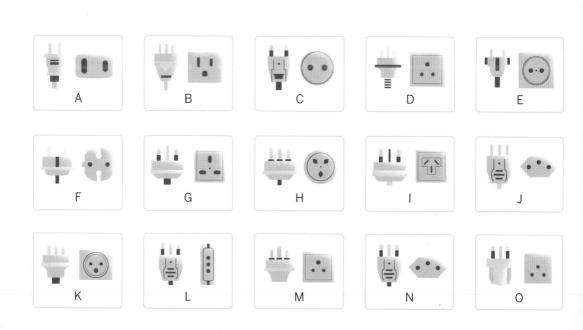

TRAVEL
HACKS

FIRST-AID KIT CHECKLIST
No one plans for holiday mishaps, but it pays to be prepared with some first aid items – here are some ideas of what to bring

- [ ] Any prescription medicines, including malaria prevention if necessary
- [ ] Paracetamol or aspirin for pain or fever, as well as an anti-inflammatory like ibuprofen
- [ ] Antidiarrhoeals for those long bus journeys
- [ ] Oral rehydration sachets
- [ ] Antihistamine tablets and cream for allergies and itching
- [ ] Sting relief spray or hydrocortisone for insect bites
- [ ] Sunscreen and lip salve containing sun block
- [ ] Insect repellent (DEET or plant-based)

- [ ] Motion sickness remedies
- [ ] Water-purifying tablets
- [ ] Over-the-counter cystitis treatment
- [ ] Aloe vera for sunburn and skin rashes
- [ ] Sticking plasters of various sizes
- [ ] Antiseptic wipes
- [ ] Tweezers to remove splinters and ticks
- [ ] Bandages, scissors and safety pins
- [ ] Blister kit
- [ ] Sterile kit, including needles, syringes, suture kit, cannula for giving a drip

OVER TO YOU

We asked you what your ultimate travel tip would be. And here are the best of them

Watch people: from a café, in a town square, at the city park. I love to see the characters each place has to offer.

@hungrytrek

Choose your travel companion(s) veeeeeeery carefully.

@KadiKaljuste

Always bring cable ties.

@fancy_clancy

If things go wrong or you make a fool of yourself it will probably make for a good story later!

Richard Boot, via Facebook

Toilet roll!!!

Chris Aggerdoo, via Facebook

Be kind. Kindness opens all doors.

Guiliana Reis,
via Facebook

Baby wipes. Always have baby wipes.

Sarah Nolan,
via Facebook

Bring a carry-on with clothes and bare necessities. If your luggage is lost your adventure doesn't have to be delayed.

@AmyErikson

Take a cab until you can see your destination in the distance, then get out and walk the rest of the way. You'll discover a lot more.

@jSteies

Eat where the locals eat.

Tom McKenna,
via Facebook

125

INDEX

ACKNOWLEDGEMENTS

The biggest thanks go to the wide range of experts, bloggers and travel professionals who gave up their time to contribute to this book, and to those incredibly helpful people who put me in touch with them. I am also grateful to Jess Cole and Dan Tucker who have been such superb colleagues to work with on this book, and to everyone in Lonely Planet's London office who has also offered support and advice. Lastly, thanks to Imogen Hall for the help and constant inspiration.

PUBLISHING DIRECTOR Piers Pickard
COMMISSIONING EDITOR Jessica Cole
ART DIRECTION & DESIGN Daniel Tucker
LAYOUT DESIGNER James Hardy
ILLUSTRATOR Crush
PRINT PRODUCTION Larissa Frost
THANKS TO Brendan Dempsey

Published in October 2014 by Lonely Planet Publications Pty Ltd
ABN 36 005 607 983
www.lonelyplanet.com
ISBN 978 1 74360 361 1
© Lonely Planet 2014
Printed in China
10 9 8 7 6 5 4 3 2 1

LONELY PLANET OFFICES

Australia 90 Maribyrnong St, Footscray, Victoria, 3011, Australia
Phone 03 8379 8000 Email talk2us@lonelyplanet.com.au

USA 150 Linden St, Oakland, CA 94607
Phone 510 250 6400 Email info@lonelyplanet.com

United kingdom Media Centre, 201 Wood Lane, London W12 7TQ
Phone 020 8433 1333 Email go@lonelyplanet.co.uk

MIX
Paper from responsible sources
FSC™ C021741

Paper in this book is certified against the Forest Stewardship Council™ standards. FSC™ promotes environmentally responsible, socially beneficial and economically viable management of the world's forests.